TAKING UP YOUR CROSS

JOHN T. MARTIN

ISBN 978-1-64349-315-2 (paperback)
ISBN 978-1-64349-316-9 (digital)

Christian Faith Publishing, Inc.
832 Park Avenue
Meadville, PA 16335
www.christianfaithpublishing.com

Printed in the United States of America

INTRODUCTION

HOLY SPIRIT–LED BOOK ON following and walking with Christ daily.

In this book, we will talk about what it truly means to take up your cross and walk with Christ daily. You will learn several different things that are essential to your relationship, fellowship, and daily walk with Christ.

> *"That which we have seen and heard declare we unto you, that ye also may have fellowship with us: and truly our fellowship is with the Father, and with his Son Jesus Christ." (1 John 1:3, KJV)*

CHAPTER 1

Taking Up Your Cross

FOLLOWING CHRIST ISN'T EASY. Jesus said in *Luke 9:23 (KJV)*, *"And he said to them all, If any man will come after me, let him deny himself, and take up his cross daily, and follow me."* Following Christ isn't always an easy life. When you really decide to follow Christ with your whole heart, you will run into road blocks, lose friends, and a lot of the time, be hated by the world along the way.

Although you will learn that when you can walk with Jesus in both the good times and in the bad times is when you are really walking with Him. When you can have joy in the good times of life and in your trials of life is when your walk will begin to mature greatly with Him! Sometimes, you will go through trials and seasons of life, where God will begin to rid you of sin. Sin that you may have been dealing with for a long time in order for you to produce more righteous fruit of the Holy Spirit's love and be a better Christ-like example of Him.

Jesus said in *John 15:2 (KJV)*, *"Every branch in me that beareth not fruit he taketh away: and every branch that beareth fruit, he purgeth it, that it may bring forth more fruit."* So sometimes, God purges us from old sin so we can be better examples for Him because he has a greater plan for our life and wants to use us in a big way. He can't use us to our fullest potential in Him until he purges us from our sins of the flesh that we may be dealing with and therefore hindering us from our fullest potential in Him! The reason is because Christ has called us to be lights for him in this world. When we are the light, we no longer live a lifestyle of sin but live to our fullest potential in Him.

Follow the Straight and Narrow

"Because strait is the gate, and narrow is the way, which leadeth unto life, and few there be that find it." (Matthew 7:14, KJV)

CHAPTER 2

You Are the Light of the World

IF YOU FOLLOW MY ministry @thelastdays777 on Instagram, a lot of times you will hear me say, "How can we be lights for the world… if we're like the world?" We have to be a set-apart people as we're called to be in order for the world to see Christ in us. We have to be different! Jesus said we are the light of the world in the book of Matthew when he said in *Matthew 5:14–16 (KJV)*, *"Ye are the light of the world. A city that is set on an hill cannot be hid. Neither do men light a candle, and put it under a bushel, but on a candlestick; and it giveth light unto all that are in the house. Let your light so shine before men, that they may see your good works, and glorify your Father which is in heaven."*

The Lord Jesus is the light of the world as mentioned in John 8:12 (KJV). Although now that the Lord Jesus is with the Father, Jesus is light of the world through us! When you walk into a room of people wherever you go, people need to see that there is something different about you, they need to see Christ in you. Also, we should never be ashamed to spread the Gospel of Christ to any person we may encounter that does not know Christ. As Apostle Paul said in *Romans 1:16 (KJV)*, *"For I am not ashamed of the gospel of Christ: for it is the power of God unto salvation to every one that believeth; to the Jew first, and also to the Greek."* We are called to spread the Gospel of Christ and be lights for the world as believers in Christ. It is our goal in life to be "fishers of men" as Jesus said in *Matthew 4:19 (KJV)*, *"And he saith unto them, Follow me, and I will make you fishers of men."* Although how can we do that if the world does not see Jesus in us? Again, we have to be different.

Walk as Children of Light

> *"For ye were sometimes darkness, but now are ye light in the Lord: walk as children of light: For the fruit of the Spirit is in all goodness and righteousness and truth."* (Ephesians 5:8–9, KJV)

CHAPTER 3

Spreading the Love of Christ

IN THE PRIOR CHAPTER, I talked about how we are called to be lights for the world. The way we do that is by being the best example of Christ we can be, by spreading the love of Christ with the world. The Lord Jesus said in the book of Matthew that the two greatest commandments are to first, love God, then second, love your neighbor as yourself, when he said in *Matthew 22:36–40 (KJV), "Master, which is the great commandment in the law? Jesus said unto him, Thou shalt love the Lord thy God with all thy heart, and with all thy soul, and with all thy mind. This is the first and great commandment. And the second is like unto it, Thou shalt love thy neighbour as thyself. On these two commandments hang all the law and the prophets."* In the book of 1 John, John also mentions that we should love one another because love is of God, when the Word says in *1 John 4:7–11 (KJV), "Beloved, let us love one another: for love is of God; and every one that loveth is born of God, and knoweth God. He that loveth not knoweth not God;*

for God is love. In this was manifested the love of God toward us, because that God sent his only begotten Son into the world, that we might live through him. Herein is love, not that we loved God, but that he loved us, and sent his Son to be the propitiation for our sins. Beloved, if God so loved us, we ought also to love one another." We are to love one another because God first loved us by sending Christ his only son to die for us so that we could be saved. We also are to love one another like Christ loved us so that the world might know the true love of Christ and be saved.

The Apostle Paul also mentions in 1 Corinthians 13 that the most important thing we could have is love, when he mentions in *1 Corinthians 13:1–3 (KJV),* "*Though I speak with the tongues of men and of angels, and have not charity, I am become as sounding brass, or a tinkling cymbal. And though I have the gift of prophecy, and understand all mysteries, and all knowledge; and though I have all faith, so that I could remove mountains, and have not charity, I am nothing. And though I bestow all my goods to feed the poor, and though I give my body to be burned, and have not charity, it profiteth me nothing.*"

He then goes on to describe the very essence of love, when he mentions in *1 Corinthians 13:4–7 (KJV),* "*Charity suffereth long, and is kind; charity envieth not; charity vaunteth not itself, is not puffed up, Doth not behave itself unseemly, seeketh not her own, is not easily provoked, thinketh no evil; Rejoiceth not in iniquity, but rejoiceth in the truth; Beareth all things, believeth all things, hopeth all things, endureth all things.*"

Paul then ends the chapter by stating that out of faith, hope, and love, the greatest of these is love, when he states in *1 Corinthians 13:13 (KJV),* "*And now abideth faith, hope, charity, these three; but the greatest of these is charity.*"

As we can see, without love, we are nothing! The Lord Jesus even said in the book of John that without Him, we can do nothing! When Jesus stated in *John 15:5 (KJV)*, *"I am the vine, ye are the branches: He that abideth in me, and I in him, the same bringeth forth much fruit: for without me ye can do nothing."* So again, as we can see, without the Lord Jesus, we have no love! The Greek word that describes the true love we receive from Jesus that is not of this world is "agape," and it means "brotherly love, affection, good will, love, benevolence." This word is used throughout the New Testament many times to describe the true love that we receive from the Lord Jesus. So when it comes down to it, how is the world going to really know Christ if we are not being examples of Him, by spreading His love with the world? Jesus even said that the world would know we are His disciples by loving one another when He stated in *John 13:35 (KJV)*, *"By this shall all men know that ye are my disciples, if ye have love one to another."*

Love One Another

"A new commandment I give unto you, That ye love one another; as I have loved you, that ye also love one another."

(John 13:34, KJV)

CHAPTER 4

※

A New Creation: Leaving Your Life of Sin

IN THIS CHAPTER, WE will talk about how following the Lord Jesus and being born again by Christ makes you a new creation in Him. Also how being a new creation in Christ means leaving your old life of sin. Jesus states in the book of John that we must be born again to see the kingdom of heaven when He states in *John 3:3–7 (KJV)*, *"Jesus answered and said unto him, Verily, verily, I say unto thee, Except a man be born again, he cannot see the kingdom of God. Nicodemus saith unto him, How can a man be born when he is old? can he enter the second time into his mother's womb, and be born? Jesus answered, Verily, verily, I say unto thee, Except a man be born of water and of the Spirit, he cannot enter into the kingdom of God. That which is born of the flesh is flesh; and that which is born of the Spirit is spirit. Marvel not that I said unto thee, Ye must be born again."* When we are born again and saved by Christ, we become a new creation or a "new creature" as the book of 2 Corinthians says in *2 Corinthians 5:17 (KJV)*, *"Therefore if any man be in Christ, he is a new creature: old things are passed away; behold, all things are become new."* The book of Ephesians also states that we are a "new man" in God when it states in *Ephesians 4:24 (KJV)*, *"And that ye put on the new man, which after God is created in righteousness and true holiness."* When we are born again in Christ, we are baptized into Jesus's death and raised with Him in His resurrection! The book of Romans makes it clear in this when it states in *Romans 6:3–7 (KJV)*, *"Know ye not, that so many of us as were baptized into Jesus Christ were baptized into his death? Therefore we are buried with him by baptism into death: that like as Christ was raised up from the dead by the glory of the Father, even so we also should walk in newness of life. For if we have been planted together in the likeness of his death, we shall be also in the likeness of his resurrection: Knowing this, that our old man is crucified with him, that the body of sin might be destroyed, that henceforth we should not serve sin. For he that is dead is freed from sin."* It also makes it clear in *Romans 6:3–7 (KJV)* that when we are baptized and resurrected with Christ, we are free from sin and should no longer serve sin, which is the next point I want to make. After we are saved by Christ, we are called to leave our old life of sin and serve sin no longer as we are a new man in Christ, we should live as Christ lived! The book of Romans also states this when it states in *Romans 6:11 (KJV)*, *"Likewise reckon ye also yourselves to be dead indeed unto sin, but alive unto God through Jesus Christ our Lord."* Romans 6 is all about how if we are new in Christ, we should no longer live in or serve sin any longer. The reason is that sin hinders you from your fullest potential relationship you can have with Christ, the Holy Spirit, and the Father. It also hinders you from being the best example of Christ you can be to the world. Not only that, but Jesus has called us not to serve sin any longer after being saved and following Him. We are to be holy as Christ and God our Father is holy, as the Word also states in *1 Peter 1:15–16 (KJV)*, *"But as he which hath called you is holy, so be ye holy in all manner of conversation; Because it is written, Be ye holy; for I am holy."* The Greek word for "holy" there in 1 Peter 1:15–16 (KJV) is the word *hagios*, and it means "most holy thing, a saint." The origin of the Greek word for "hagios" actually comes from the Greek word "hagnos," and it means "pure from carnality, chaste, modest, pure from every fault, immaculate, clean." We also know that the Word says that God chose us through Christ before the foundation of the world to be holy and without blame before Him in love (see Ephesians 1:3–5, KJV; Colossians 1:22, KJV). So if God chose us through Christ to be holy, we should walk our lives as holy and pure servants of Christ and children of God. For the Word says in *1 Peter 2:9–10 (KJV)*, *"But ye are a chosen generation, a royal priesthood, a holy nation, a peculiar people; that ye should shew forth the praises of him who hath called you out of darkness into his marvellous light; Which in time past were not a people, but are now the people of God: which had not obtained mercy, but now have obtained mercy."* So we are a chosen generation and a holy nation through Christ to be a set apart people from the world. In order to be lights of Christ to the world, we must understand that just as Jesus was not of this world, we are not of this world but of the kingdom of heaven! I believe the Christian culture today has just settled for the excuse of "Oh, I'm just a sinner," making excuses to keep living their life in the same old sin cycles, thinking they just can't do anything about it to change their lifestyle. The reason is that they know the Lord Jesus will forgive them, so they just keep doing whatever they want to do just like the rest of the world. Don't get me wrong, I'm not saying were all perfect by any means because there was only one perfect man that ever walked this earth and that was the Lord Jesus. Although I am saying we can choose to change our lifestyle and stop walking into the same old sins on a day-to-day basis, thinking the Lord Jesus will just forgive us for it. I mean, don't get me wrong either, the Lord Jesus will forgive you because that's how good our Father God Jehovah and the Lord Jesus is, but for us to keep doing the same thing over and over again, then asking for forgiveness later? That is an abuse of the grace and forgiveness that the Lord Jesus has graciously given to us. It would do us well to remember that we don't deserve grace and forgiveness in the first place! Yes, it is an absolute fact we all have sins, and we all have fallen, and fall short of the glory of God everyday (see Romans 3:23–24, KJV; 1 John 1:9, KJV). Although we can make the choice to resist the temptation every day when those different sins come along. Again, we are called to live holy as God, Christ, and the Holy Spirit are holy, although it is our choice whether or not we choose to live as Christ has called us to be.

Put On the New Man

"And that ye put on the new man, which after God is created in righteousness and true holiness." (Ephesians 4:24, KJV)

CHAPTER 5

Persevering through Persecution

At some point in your life, you will face some sort of persecution during your walk with Christ. It may be several different ways, but you will face persecution. Jesus said in *2 Timothy 3:12 (KJV)*, *"Yea, and all that will live godly in Christ Jesus shall suffer persecution."*

Sometimes, you will suffer persecution for teaching the Word or talking about the Word with somebody who will hate you for doing so. As the Lord Jesus said in *John 15:20–21 (KJV)*, *"Remember the word that I said unto you, The servant is not greater than his lord. If they have persecuted me, they will also persecute you; if they have kept my saying, they will keep yours also. But all these things will they do unto you for my name's sake, because they know not him that sent me."*

It is in those times that you will need to keep persevering for Christ's name sake. The word *persevere* is defined as "continue in a course of action even in the face of difficulty." Although the word *perseverance* is defined as "steady persistence in a course of action, a purpose, a state, etc., especially in spite of difficulties, obstacles, or discouragement."

You will learn to persevere no matter what you face as a Christian or how much you are hated for Christ's name sake. Jesus even stated in Luke 21:17 (KJV) that you will be hated of all men for His name's sake.

"And ye shall be hated of all men for my name's sake." (Luke 21:17, KJV)

There are brothers and sisters all over the world who are daily mistreated and persecuted for being a Christian every day. According to an article from christianitytoday.com written in 2017: "Approximately 215 million Christians experience high, very high, or extreme persecution."

Know that if the world hates you, know that it hated our Lord Jesus first. The Lord Jesus even said that if the world hates you, know that it hated me before it hated you (John 15:18, KJV). Jesus then goes on to say that if you were of the world, the world would love his own: but because you are not of the world, but I have chosen you out of the world, therefore the world hates you (John 15:19, KJV).

Even if the world hates you, know you still have to keep persevering for Christ's name sake because when it comes down to it, belonging to Lord Jesus is far more precious and important than belonging to the world. This world will perish away with its sin, but we that belong to Christ will never perish, as we have the precious gift of salvation of eternal life in heaven with Christ and God's love.

When persecution comes, will we run? No. When affliction comes, will we run? No.

When hate comes, will we run? No.

We are to keep fighting the good fight no matter what may come our way. Knowing Christ will be with us no matter what we face! Jesus said He would be with us even unto the end of the world (Matthew 28:20, KJV). As the Word says in *Romans 8:31 (KJV)*, *"What shall we then say to these things? If God be for us, who can be against us?"*

During the Sermon on the Mount, one of the most famous sermons that Jesus ever taught, mentioned in Matthew 5 (KJV). Jesus is teaching on the Beatitudes. During His teaching on the Beatitudes, Jesus says, *"Blessed are they which are persecuted for righteousness sake: for theirs is the kingdom of heaven" (Matthew 5:10, KJV).*

Guys, we are the children of God, and our reward is the kingdom of heaven, what such a beautiful and amazing reward we have in Christ. Although sometimes, we will be persecuted for being children of God by being examples of Christ on this earth. However, that does not mean we should back down when persecution comes, but rather stand our ground in the hope we have in Christ. Striving to be the best examples we can be for Christ while on this earth until the Lord Jesus takes us home.

Keep fighting the good fight of faith, brothers and sisters, no matter what may come your way, knowing Jesus will be with us until the very end!

Blessed Are They Which Are Persecuted for Righteousness' Sake

"Blessed are they which are persecuted for righteousness' sake: for theirs is the kingdom of heaven." (Matthew 5:10, KJV)

CHAPTER 6

Praising and Giving
Thanks to God

A LOT OF US ARE blessed with so much: shelter, food, clean water, health, good family, clothes on our back, etc. The biggest blessing we have is salvation in our Lord Jesus Christ. Although, do we take the time to give thanks and praise God for blessing us with all those things? The answer for most of us is actually no. Why do we not take the time to praise God and give thanks to Him for all the things in our life he has blessed us with, when in reality that's all he asks for in return is praise and thanks, but yet we don't do it. It is something I think about all the time when I look at everything God has blessed me with! Also, why do we not praise and give thanks to God enough for Jesus? The fact alone that we have salvation in Jesus's name and have a way out of this world through Him? That is the biggest blessing and gift you can ever receive in your life, but yet we take it for granted. Yes, we go to church on Sundays and praise God for twenty minutes and listen to a thirty-minute sermon, but do we praise and give thanks to Him on a day-to-day basis? It is something so easy and so simple, but yet again, we don't do it.

The Word says multiple times that we should give thanks for everything in our lives to God and our Lord Jesus Christ. Here are just a few that the Word mentions:

"Giving thanks always for all things unto God and the Father in the name of our Lord Jesus Christ." (Ephesians 5:20, KJV)

"By him therefore let us offer the sacrifice of praise to God continually, that is, the fruit of [our] lips giving thanks to his name." (Hebrews 13:15, KJV)

"In every thing give thanks: for this is the will of God in Christ Jesus concerning you." (1 Thessalonians 5:18, KJV)

Why is it that we do not give thanks and praise to God on a day-to-day basis for everything that He has done for us in our lives? It is a question that I've always wondered about. We should be giving thanks and praising God on a day-to-day basis for everything He has given us in our lives. If for no other reason that we should be giving thanks and praising God for our blessings, do it because the Word says so! We have to be obedient to God, the Lord Jesus, and His Word. When were obedient to God and His Word and give thanks and praise to God, you will see more answered prayers and joy in your life. There are tons of scriptures about praising God in the Bible although these are just a few:

"Now therefore, our God, we thank thee, and praise thy glorious name." (1 Chronicles 29:13, KJV)

"O give thanks unto the LORD, for [he is] good: for his mercy [endureth] for ever." (Psalms 107:1, KJV)

"Let every thing that hath breath praise the LORD. Praise ye the LORD." (Psalms 150:6, KJV)

When we praise God and Christ for His glorious goodness, you not only will see more answered prayers in your life but more of the Holy Spirit's goodness in your life. More love, joy, peace, longsuffering, gentleness, goodness, faith, Meekness, temperance (see Galatians 5:22–23, KJV). As the righteous fruits of the Holy Spirit's love take over in your life. It is an absolutely beautiful thing. You will begin to want to praise God, Christ, and the Holy Spirit more and more every day because of the righteous fruits that the Holy Spirit will begin to produce more and more in your life. You will begin to become addicted to praising God, Christ, and the Holy Spirit's goodness because of His presence in your life! I guarantee it, when you begin to see His precious presence show up in your life more and more every day? You will praise God!

In Everything Give Thanks

"In every thing give thanks: for this is the will of God in Christ Jesus concerning you."
(1 Thessalonians 5:18, KJV)

CHAPTER 7

Christianity Isn't a Religion
It's a Faith and a Relationship

FIRST OFF, I WANT to say, when people ask me, "What religion are you?" I answer, "I don't have a religion, my faith is Christ Jesus the Lord." The reason I respond that way is because Christianity is not a religion it is a faith, a walk, and a relationship with God, Christ, and the Holy Spirit. Religion is the differences in denominations of churches. Some churches say we believe and do things this way, others say we believe and do things this way. That is religion, traditions between denominations of churches and different rules and beliefs between different denominations. Although when it comes down to it, traditions, rules, and regulations between churches are not going to save you, it is the Lord Jesus that will save you from this world. It is not about doing things a certain way in the church, it is about what the Word of God says. In the Gospel of Mark, Mark even talks about how the traditions of men make the Word of God of no effect when he says in *Mark 7:13 (KJV)*, *"Making the word of God of none effect through your tradition, which ye have delivered: and many such like things do ye."* Religion says if you don't do things this way, God won't approve or love you as much. Although we know God's love is not based on traditions of men or churches, God's love for us is unconditional, no matter how we think were supposed to do things. The rules we follow are God's rules based on what the Word says, not on what men say we should or shouldn't do. Look at the Pharisees for example. The Pharisees were the religious rulers of Jesus's day. They were constantly threatening and hassling Jesus for what He was doing. They were so obsessed with religion that they missed the point of what Jesus was doing! Jesus did not come religiously minded. He came in love and with what God said, not on what religion said. That is why He was so hated by the Pharisees and religious people of His day because he didn't come doing what men said He should do. He came doing what God said He should do, and He was hated because of it. We should be the same way, not following what men and denominations say we should do, but what God and the Lord Jesus say we should do based on what the Word of God says.

So why do we have the Word? We have the Word of God in order to fellowship with God, Christ, and the Holy Spirit, in order to find the answers to the problems of life through what God said. We have the Word to grow with Christ and mature with Christ in His Word. Then finally we have the Word to spread the Gospel of Christ. It's like this, when you're growing up, you ask your parent the question to a problem, and your parent replies, "Son, I've already told you once, I'm not going to tell you again." It's the same thing as that. God has already given us the Word to fellowship with Him, but also that we may know the answers to the problems in our life. God wants to fellowship with us;

it's a relationship. Christianity is not a religion, it is a faith and walk with God and Christ. As you grow with Christ, you will face obstacles, but you have the Word to rely on what God said and what Christ said and what the Holy Spirit said to find comfort you, in those obstacles, trials, and tribulations. Although know this, if God brings you to it, God will bring you through it. He will hold your hand all the way through it and comfort you in it. As the Word says in *Isaiah 41:10 (KJV)*, *"Fear thou not; for I am with thee: be not dismayed; for I am thy God: I will strengthen thee; yea, I will help thee; yea, I will uphold thee with the right hand of my righteousness."* We do not need to come to God with just our problems, we need to come to God on a day-to-day basis in prayer. As Apostle Paul stated in *1 Thessalonians 5:17 (KJV)*, *"Pray without ceasing."* Now that does not mean praying one big prayer without stopping, it means constantly be talking and praying to God every day in your lives about everything conversational. Whether you are going through a storm in your life or whether you are just driving to the grocery store, include God, Christ, and the Holy Spirit in everything you do! When you do that, you will notice a huge impact on your life. As God will show up in every aspect of your life when you are constantly talking and praying to Him every day throughout your day and fellowshipping with Him in His Word. As He wants all of us so badly to do, that is why we have the Word. As a marriage is a relationship, so it is with God and with Christ with us. We have to walk with them in the good times, and in the bad times, in sickness, and in health. Knowing that we will overcome every obstacle in our lives because God and the Lord Jesus is on and by our side! We all have our problems in life, and God knows that, but He will be faithful to make us overcome every problem in our lives if we would just walk with Him, trust in Him, and fellowship with Him in His Word.

We as humans were made for relationships, God made us as relational beings. He did that for a purpose, and it is because He wants us to be in relationship with Him. That is the whole point of our lives is to be in relationship with Him. See God knew we could not survive on our own, He knew we needed help that is why He made us to be in relationship with Him and to rely on Him with our lives because He loves us. He loves us so much that He sent His only son, the Lord Jesus to die for us so that we could be in relationship with Him and be saved from this awful world!

Starting off in the very beginning, God created Adam and Eve to be in a relationship with Him forever. We as humans were never supposed to die. Then once Adam and Eve fell, death and sin came into the picture, and God was then separated from mankind because of sin and death. Although God already had the Lord Jesus ready to come and save us from this world so we could be in relationship with Him again. We know God had the Lord Jesus ready even at that point because the Word says in 1 Peter 1:19–20 (KJV) that Jesus was the lamb foreordained before the foundation of the world but was manifest in these last times for us.

"But with the precious blood of Christ, as of a lamb without blemish and without spot: Who verily was foreordained before the foundation of the world, but was manifest in these last times for you." (1 Peter 1:19–20, KJV)

God wanted to be in relationship with us so badly that He sent Jesus so we could be in relationship with Him again in heaven forever. Our hope and relationship with God, Jesus, and the Holy Spirit is the most precious thing in the world, knowing that someday we will be with them again forever in heaven. Knowing that in heaven, there will be no more death, sorrow, crying, or pain like the Word says in Revelation 21.

"And God shall wipe away all tears from their eyes; and there shall be no more death, neither sorrow, nor crying, neither shall there be any more pain: for the former things are passed away. And he that sat upon the throne said, Behold, I make all things new. And he said unto me, Write: for these words are true and faithful." (Revelation 21:4–5, KJV)

God will make all things new, and our relationship with Him will be forever in love in heaven!

Fellowship with God and the Lord Jesus

"God is faithful, by whom ye were called unto the fellowship of his Son Jesus Christ our Lord." (1 Corinthians 1:9, KJV)

CHAPTER 8

The Power of the Cross:
The Sacrifice for Sin

When we think about the power of the cross, we know that it represented the sacrifice of sin for all mankind, as Jesus so graciously died for our sins so that we could be saved. Apostle Paul even knew that there was power in the cross when He talked about the power of God in the cross in *1 Corinthians 1:18 (KJV), "For the preaching of the cross is to them that perish foolishness; but unto us which are saved it is the power of God."*

If you take a look at the meaning of biblical numbers in the Bible, it is an interesting study. First off looking at the meaning of the number 6. The number 6 in the Bible represents or means "sin" or "man." Jesus came as a "man" for the sacrifice of "sins" for mankind. Being the only begotten son of God. If you look at the Word in Mark 15:33 (KJV) Jesus was on the cross on the "sixth" hour, and it says that in the "sixth" hour, there was darkness over the whole land until the ninth hour. The darkness over the whole land represented the darkness of "sin" of mankind. Again, Jesus being on the cross in the "sixth" hour as well represented the sacrifice for the "sin" of mankind. Next, if you take a look at the meaning of the number 9, it means or represents "finality" or "judgment." Again looking at Mark 15:33 (KJV), it says that in the sixth hour there was darkness over the whole land until the "ninth" hour. It was then in the "ninth" hour in Mark 15:37–38 (KJV) that Jesus then gave up the ghost and died on the cross, representing the "final" sacrifice for the "sin" of mankind. It is an interesting revelation that you otherwise would not know unless you studied the meaning of biblical numbers in the Bible.

The writer of the book of Hebrews, believed to be the Apostle Paul, mentions a great point about Jesus being the perfect sacrifice for the sins of mankind. As the Word states in *Hebrews 9:26–28 (KJV)*, *"For then must he often have suffered since the foundation of the world: but now once in the end of the world hath he appeared to put away sin by the sacrifice of himself. And as it is appointed unto men once to die, but after this the judgment: So Christ was once offered to bear the sins of many; and unto them that look for him shall he appear the second time without sin unto salvation."*

Jesus being the final sacrifice for the sins of mankind meant that man no longer had to make any more sacrifices to God for their sins, as they did in the Old Testament through the blood of animals. This point is made very clear in the book of Hebrews also when the Word states:

"But in those sacrifices there is a remembrance again made of sins every year. For it is not possible that the blood of bulls and of goats should take away sins. Wherefore when he cometh into the world, he saith, Sacrifice and offering thou wouldest not, but

a body hast thou prepared me: In burnt offerings and sacrifices for sin thou hast had no pleasure." (Hebrews 10:3–6, KJV)

"And every priest standeth daily ministering and offering oftentimes the same sacrifices, which can never take away sins: But this man, after he had offered one sacrifice for sins for ever, sat down on the right hand of God." (Hebrews 10:11–12, KJV)

He then sums it up by saying in *Hebrews 10:17–18 (KJV), "And their sins and iniquities will I remember no more. Now where remission of these is, there is no more offering for sin."* So Jesus fulfilled God's will for us to be saved from sin by offering the Lord Jesus as the final sacrifice for all the sins of mankind. Making it possible that no more sacrifices needed to be done because our Lord Jesus Christ was the final sacrifice for all the sins of mankind. There is power in the cross, the power of God, saving us from our sins and from the world!

The Power of the Cross

"For the preaching of the cross is to them that perish foolishness; but unto us which are saved it is the power of God." (1 Corinthians 1:18, KJV)

CHAPTER 9

Facing Giants, Trials, Tribulations, and Seasons of Storms in Your Life, as You Await God's Blessing for Your Life

IF YOU LOOK AT the Old Testament, the Israelites had to face so many obstacles and roadblocks on their way to their promised blessing of the Promised Land or Israel. The Israelites faced armies and armies of giants before they got to the Promised Land. You know they had to be anxious and scared, but God was faithful to conquer and take down every roadblock of giants that stood in their way. The reason is because God had great plans in mind for the Israelites. He wanted to bless them so much as they were God's chosen people.

Sometimes, you will face giants, obstacles, and road-blocks in your life. Seasons of storms, trials, and tribulations. Although know that God will take down every giant, roadblock, and obstacle that stands in your way. Why is that you ask? The reason is because God has great plans for your life. God wants to bless His children with a great future full of hope, and life. As the prophet Jeremiah said in *Jeremiah 29:11 (KJV)*, *"For I know the thoughts that I think toward you, saith the Lord, thoughts of peace, and not of evil, to give you an expected end."*

You will notice, too, during the seasons of storms in your life that the love of the Holy Spirit will begin to teach you to be patient during your trials. You will learn much patience as you await your promised blessing from God in your life. You will also learn hope and faith, as you rely on God and the Lord Jesus to take down the roadblocks, obstacles, and giants that you face. Although that patience, hope, and faith will pay off when you finally receive the blessing and plans that God has for you in your life. The Apostle Paul stated in *Romans 5:3–4 (KJV)*, *"And not only so, but we glory in tribulations also: knowing that tribulation worketh patience; And patience, experience; and experience, hope."*

We should have hope knowing that God will provide a way out of every situation we face and get us to the other side. Even in fearful situations, have hope because God and the Lord Jesus will calm every storm in your life. If you look at Mark 4:35–41 (KJV), the disciples of our Lord Jesus were in a great storm while on their boat. They were so afraid and thought they weren't going to make it. Even before the storm the Lord Jesus said, "Let us pass over unto the other side." See, Jesus already knew the storm was coming before it even happened, but He also knew that they would make it through the storm and to the other side. Even still though the disciples were so terrified of the storm, but Jesus, sleeping in the boat, just stood up and rebuked the wind and said unto the sea, "Peace, be still" and calmed the storm. He then asked the disciples why they were so fearful and why they had no faith? The disciples then realized Jesus, was in control of everything!

We should look at our spiritual storms, the same way we look at physical storms outside. We see a storm coming and we say, "Oh, it is about to storm." Although we know it will rain for a little bit, thunder, and lightning for a little while, it will pass and everything will be fine again. That's the way we should look at our spiritual storms in our lives. Knowing it will storm for a little while but eventually, all will be calm again and everything will be fine again. Jesus will calm every storm we face in our lives.

I have faced much adversity and many storms in my life. There were times when I didn't think I was going to make it, but even then, Jesus calmed every one. Jesus has held my hand through each storm, roadblock, obstacle, and giant that I have faced in my life. I'll also say that storms are not very much fun but know it is only to make you stronger in Christ! I found my faith, hope, and patience increase tremendously, as I relied on the Lord Jesus to make a way, when I thought there was no way. There were some days that I felt so overwhelmed that I did not think I would make it through the moment, day, or the next day! I would just say, "Lord Jesus, I know you will deliver me and make a way for me," and the Lord Jesus would do exactly that. Daily miracles I have experienced in my life as I saw the Lord Jesus show up when everything looked like it was coming to an end! I would cry out to the Lord Jesus with tears running down my face and say, "Jesus, I need you now!" and instantly, the storm would calm. It was absolutely amazing and no better feeling knowing He is near! Sometimes, the Lord Jesus will allow you to go through things in your life in order for Him to come to you and show up in a way that you have never seen before. It is in those trials and seasons of storms in your life, when you are absolutely at your wits' end, that Jesus will come through in a new and amazing way. He will show up in your life like never before. It will absolutely amaze you and tremendously increase your faith in Christ. It was in the times that I felt out of control that I learned Jesus was ultimately in control. God and the Lord Jesus will hold your hand and deliver you from every situation you will face in your life!

As you await your promised blessing of God's plans for your life, know that on the straight and narrow path of walking with Christ, God will take down and conquer everything that stands in your way. Never give up, never lose hope, keep fighting the good fight of faith, and trust God with every step in your life, and He will bring you your promised blessing of His plans for you!

We Glory in Tribulations

"And not only so, but we glory in tribulations also: knowing that tribulation worketh patience; And patience, experience; and experience, hope." (Romans 5:3–4, KJV)

33

Chapter 10

Daily Repentance and
Avoiding Sin

Repentance is a very important part of our walk with Christ. Repentance is defined as "sincere regret or remorse," although the Bible defines it from the Greek word *metanoeo* and it means "to change one's mind for the better, heartily to amend with abhorrence of one's past sins." When we sin, we should be genuinely sorry for the sins we commit and turn from them and learn from them and not make the same mistake again.

You will notice when you commit a sin, your joy in Christ will instantly fade and shame, regret, and guilt will set in. Although that actually is a good thing because it is the Holy Spirit convicting you to immediately repent those sins and be forgiven by Christ. We also know that Lord Jesus said in John 16:8 (KJV) that the Holy Spirit would convict us of sin when the Holy Spirit came. We also know that in 2 Corinthians 7:9–10 (KJV), it talks about how Godly sorrow brings repentance but worldly sorrow brings death. It is a bad thing if you feel no regret, shame, or guilt after you commit a sin because that means you have become hardened to sin and that is a terrible thing because it affects the fullness of your walk with God and Christ, when your heart becomes hardened to the Holy Spirit and God.

When we sin, we immediately need to repent and get those sins forgiven. If you sit in your sins for days and days on end and don't repent them, your joy in Christ will stay lowered, and bitterness, depression, shame, and guilt will set in and your walk with Christ will not be at its fullest potential. The Word says in 1 John 1:9 (KJV) that if we confess our sins, He is faithful and just to forgive us our sins and to cleanse us from all unrighteousness.

We should try to avoid sin at all costs, not only because God and Christ said so but also because it effects the fullness of our walk with Christ that you can have. When you try to avoid sin and not walk in sin but be led by the Holy Spirit, you will notice Christ's presence way more in every way in your life when you don't let the burden of sin bring it down constantly.

There are all kinds of sins and we know that as the Word clearly states. Although we also know that we have been freed from the law of sin and death, as the Word also clearly states in Romans 8:2 (KJV). We should walk with Christ in that mind-set that we have already been made free from sin, because of Christ sacrifice for us on the cross. Romans 6 (KJV) is a great chapter to read as well, that talks about how we have been made free from sin and should no longer serve sin, but live unto God and Christ.

I do want to make this point very clear as well though when I say that of course we are not perfect. There is only one perfect man that ever walked this earth and that was the Lord Jesus Christ. We also know that the Word states in Romans 3:23 (KJV) that all have sinned and come short of the glory of God. We are not perfect people, but we should do our very best to live like Christ, as Christ has called us to do, and that means leaving sin behind and doing our very best to try to avoid it.

Daily repentance is very important because it keeps us on a clean slate and refreshed with God everyday with our walk with Him. The Word also states in 2 Corinthians 4:16 (KJV) that though our outward man perish, yet the inward man is renewed day by day.

See God wants to walk and fellowship with you every day with such a great joy and love in Him that you would have no need to turn to sin to try to find happiness, love, and joy. God wants to give you true love and joy that only comes from Him, Christ, and the Holy Spirit and not of this world.

Daily repentance keeps your joy in Christ up and keeps you right and clean before God and Christ every day.

God Will Remember Our Sins No More

"For I will be merciful to their unrighteousness, and their sins and their iniquities will I remember no more." (Hebrews 8:12, KJV)

CHAPTER 11

Forgiving One Another

WHEN IT COMES TO forgiving one another, we know it is very important. First off, our Lord Jesus stated in Matthew 6:14–15 (KJV) that if we forgive men their sins, our heavenly Father will also forgive us. But if we do not forgive men their sins, neither will our Father forgive us. So as you can see it is very important that we forgive others for their sins in order for us to be forgiven also.

I know sometimes it is hard to forgive somebody that has done you wrong. It can be tough letting go of anger and grudges that you have for somebody, but at the end of the day, it only hurts you more. The reason for that is because when you hold on to grudges against somebody, it only produces bitterness inside of you, and bitterness is a terrible thing to be filled with. Bitterness tears you down in many ways, but the most important thing it affects is your relationship, joy, and general happiness in Christ.

The Word states in Ephesians 4:26 (KJV) to "let not the sun go down upon your wrath."

That means do not go to bed angry with any unresolved problems that you may be facing against somebody. Resolve any problems you have with somebody and forgive them for what they have done to you. When you forgive them of their sins against you, you will notice that anger and bitterness will leave you, and you will feel such a relief and peace. *Ephesians 4:31–32 (KJV) also says to "Let all bitterness, and wrath, and anger, and clamour, and evil speaking, be put away from you, with all malice: And be ye kind one to another, tenderhearted, forgiving one another, even as God for Christ's sake hath forgiven you."*

We are called to forgive one another even as God in Christ has forgiven us.

Jesus talks about in *Luke 17:3–4 (KJV) that "If thy brother trespass against thee, rebuke him; and if he repent, forgive him. And if he trespass against thee seven times in a day, and seven times in a day turn again to thee, saying, I repent; thou shalt forgive him."* Again remembering what Jesus said in Matthew 6:14–15 (KJV) that if we forgive men for their sins against us, God will forgive our sins also.

Forgive If You Have Anything Against Anyone

"And when ye stand praying, forgive, if ye have ought against any: that your Father also which is in heaven may forgive you your trespasses." (Mark 11:25, KJV)

CHAPTER 12

---◇◇◇---

The Power and Action of Praying Scripture to God

IN THIS CHAPTER, WE will look at the power and action of praying scripture to God. We know the Word of God is a literal weapon, so also is the action of praying it to God, in whatever situation or problem we might be going through. The action of praying scripture to God is very powerful and can be used for all our daily battles and struggles.

First, when you begin to pray scripture to God, it reassures us that He said it and put it there for a purpose. That purpose is not only for you to learn from, but for you to use in prayer with Him. When we find ourselves praying routine or chore-like prayers, our Father God has given us an example of how we should communicate with him. We find this example in the book of Matthew when Jesus is teaching on prayer and states in *Matthew 6:8–13 (KJV), "Be not ye therefore like unto them: for your Father knoweth what things ye have need of, before ye ask him. After this manner therefore pray ye:*

Our Father which art in heaven, Hallowed be thy name. Thy kingdom come. Thy will be done in earth, as it is in heaven. Give us this day our daily bread. And forgive us our debts, as we forgive our debtors. And lead us not into temptation, but deliver us from evil: For thine is the kingdom, and the power, and the glory, for ever. A'-men."

As we know, God does not contradict His Word, nor will he ever contradict His Word. He never changes and we know that as a fact! We can reference that fact in several different scriptures. The first one that I like is in the book of Malachi when the Word of God states in *Malachi 3:6 (KJV),* *"For I am the LORD, I change not; therefore ye sons of Jacob are not consumed."* Another one is in the book of Psalms when the Word of God states in *Psalms 102:27 (KJV),* *"But thou art the same, and thy years shall have no end."* We also know as fact that as God never changes or passes away, neither does His Word! We can reference to that fact in scripture as well. In the book of Matthew chapter 24 states, the Word states, *"Heaven and earth shall pass away, but my words shall not pass away"* *(Matthew 24:35, KJV).* Another great verse is in the book of Psalms, when the Word states in *Psalms 119:89 (KJV),* *"For ever, O LORD, thy word is settled in heaven."* If we look at the Hebrew word for *heaven* used in *Psalms 119:89,* that word is *shamayim,* and it is used in the context of *"Heaven as the abode of God"* or in a simple translation, the kingdom of God. As we know the first two heavens will pass away with a *"fervent heat"* during *"the day of the Lord,"* as stated in *2 Peter 3:10 (KJV).*

Secondly, the Word of God has power when we pray it to God Himself and let God carry it out upon our request! We can be reminded of that fact if we reference the book of Isaiah chapter 55, *"So shall my word be that goeth forth out of my mouth: it shall not return unto me void, but it shall accomplish that which I please, and it shall prosper in the thing whereto I sent it" (Isaiah 55:11, KJV).* The Lord even tells us that through the apostle Paul in 2 Timothy, to remind other brothers and sisters of that as well. The Word states in *2 Timothy 2:14 (KJV), "Of these things put them in remembrance charging them before the Lord that they strive not about words to no profit, but to the subverting of the hearers."*

So with that being said, it is here where we begin to dig into and discuss what the act of praying the Word of God really means, and why it is important for us to not only pray, but to pray the words of God from the Word of God instead of praying out of our own words. I will begin this point by starting out with a verse spoken by Jesus in the book of Matthew chapter 4, when he too quoted scripture. The Word states, *"But he answered and said, it is written, Man shall not live by bread alone, but by every word that proceedeth out of the mouth of God" (Matthew 4:4, KJV)* Our Lord and Savior Jesus Christ tells us in the book of Matthew that whatever we ask in prayer, believe, and we shall receive it, when the Word states in *Matthew 21:22 (KJV), "And all things, whatsoever ye shall ask in prayer, believing, ye shall receive."* Although whatever we may be asking in prayer, we also have to ask and pray with faith and confidence that God will hear us and answer it. The Word says in *Hebrews 11:6 (KJV), "But without faith it is impossible to please him: for he that cometh to God must believe that he is, and that he is a rewarder of them that diligently seek him."* The book of Romans states in *Romans 8:15 (KJV), "For ye have not received the spirit of bondage again to fear; but ye have received the Spirit of adoption, whereby we cry, Ab'-ba, Father."*

It is just as important to remember that when we pray, we are not only just praying to God, we are praying to our literal Father in heaven! So with that being said, we have to look at prayer, as not just words that come out of our mouths, but we have to look at it and know that we are having a literal conversation with our Father who cares and loves us deeply and more than we could ever know!

Here is an example of what I'm talking about. Let's say that I've been struggling with fear lately and have been struggling with it hard. Then, in that situation, I would open up my Bible to specific scriptures that talk about fear, and I would start to pray those literal scriptures to God and say: "Father, you know lately that I have been struggling majorly with fear. Father I know we don't have the Spirit of fear because your Word states in *2 Timothy 1:7 (KJV)*, "*For God hath not given us the spirit of fear; but of power, and of love, and of a sound mind.*" I know this Father because your Word also states in *1 John 4:18 (KJV)*, "*There is no fear in love; but perfect love casteth out fear: because fear hath torment. He that feareth is not made perfect in love.*" Although, Father, I know I have been made perfect in love by the blood of Jesus Christ my Lord and Savior. So, Father, right now, I am just commanding these false feelings and lies, to leave me in the name of Jesus! I also command it with the authority given to me by my Lord and Savior Jesus Christ Himself, according to what your Word says Father, in the book of *Luke* chapter 10, when Jesus states, "*Behold, I give unto you power to tread on serpents and scorpions, and over all the power of the enemy: and nothing shall by any means hurt you. Notwithstanding in this rejoice not, that the spirits are subject unto you; but rather rejoice, because your names are written in heaven*" (*Luke 10:19–20, KJV*). Then finally, Father, I claim this victory and answered prayer also, with what your Word also says Father, in the book of *John* chapter 14, when Jesus also states, "*And whatsoever ye shall ask in my name, that will I do, that the Father may be glorified in the Son. If ye shall ask any thing in my name, I will do it" (John 14:13–14, KJV)*. So, Father, in the name of my Lord and Savior Jesus Christ, do I claim this promise and authority right now, that you may be glorified through your first born Son, Jesus Christ our Lord and Savior and King, according to your Word, Amen!"

With that example, you can see how praying God's Word can change your prayer life and your relationship with God our Father and with our Lord and Savior Jesus Christ tremendously! We have to believe, too, when we begin to pray for whatever we are going through, that the Father and our Lord and Savior Jesus Christ want to help us in our times of need! We know that because of several scriptures, but one in particular says in the book of Hebrews, about coming before the "throne of grace" in our "time of need": *"For we have not an high priest which cannot be touched with the feeling of our infirmities; but was in all points tempted like as we are, yet without sin. Let us therefore come boldly unto the throne of grace, that we may obtain mercy, and find grace to help in time of need"* (Hebrews 4:15–16, KJV). Also, if you take a look at the Greek strong for the word *infirmities* there, it's actually the word *astheneia*, and it can mean "want of strength," "weakness," "its native weakness and frailty," "feebleness of health or sickness." Although if you dig a little deeper into the root word of *astheneia*, which is *sthenoo*, it can actually mean "to make strong," "strengthen (of one's soul)."

The Father in heaven has given us His Word for a purpose, and that purpose is for us to use it in relationship with Him and Jesus Christ. Again, we can know this by scripture. In 2 Timothy, the Word of God states, *"But continue thou in the things which thou hast learned and hast been assured of, knowing of whom thou hast learned them; And that from a child thou hast known the holy scriptures, which are able to make thee wise unto salvation through faith which is in Christ Jesus. All scripture is given by inspiration of God, and is profitable for doctrine, for reproof, for correction, for instruction in righteousness"* *(2 Timothy 3:14–16, KJV).*

In conclusion, we can see that God gave us His Word for a purpose, knowing that we would need it for everything in our everyday lives, including praying it to Him. That is why He took so much time throughout many generations of chosen people to keep it and put it all together for us to use! Lastly, it is so very important that we stay close to God and His Word. In doing this, we will know exactly where to go in His Word for what we may need to know from His Word!

The Word of God Is a Literal Weapon

> *"For the word of God is quick, and powerful, and sharper than any two-edged sword, piercing even to the dividing asunder of soul and spirit, and of the joints and marrow, and is a discerner of the thoughts and intents of the heart." (Hebrews 4:12, KJV)*

CHAPTER 13

The Love Dove Language:
Praying in the Holy Spirit!

The Difference between Speaking with Diverse Tongues and the Prayer Language of the Holy Spirit

FIRST OFF, I WANT to say that our Lord Jesus Himself said in *Mark 16:17* that we as believers would speak with "new tongues" when He said in *Mark 16:17–18, "And these signs shall follow them that believe; In my name shall they cast out devils; they shall speak with new tongues; They shall take up serpents; and if they drink any deadly thing, it shall not hurt them; they shall lay hands on the sick, and they shall recover."* Although there is a difference between praying in the Holy Spirit's prayer language tongue and speaking with diverse tongues. When you pray in the Holy Spirit, you are speaking in an unknown tongue not diverse tongues as mentioned in

1 Corinthians 12:7–11. Apostle Paul does not mention in *1 Corinthians 12:7–11*, when he mentions the manifestation gifts of the Holy Spirit speaking in an unknown tongue, he only mentions speaking in diverse tongues because there is a difference. Although praying in the Holy Spirit is still the Holy Spirit manifesting through you as you pray to God.

When you are praying in the Holy Spirit, you are speaking in an unknown tongue given directly from Father God Jehovah Himself for prayer. An unknown tongue is not a diverse tongue as mentioned in *1 Corinthians 12:7–11*, it is a separate tongue given for prayer between you and God. Diverse tongues are earthly languages of the world as in English, Hebrew, or Spanish, etc. Diverse tongues are what the disciples of Jesus spoke with on the Day of Pentecost in (Acts 2) when the Holy Spirit first came.

If you look at the Greek word for "diverse tongues" mentioned in 1 Corinthians 12:10 (KJV), it is the word *genos,* and it means "kindred, stock, tribe, nation, nationality or descent from a particular people." So they are earthly languages of the nations of the world. If you then look at *1 Corinthians 14,* Apostle Paul first mentions speaking in an unknown tongue in *1 Corinthians 14:2 (KJV), "For he that speaketh in an unknown tongue speaketh not unto men, but unto God: for no man understandeth him; howbeit in the spirit he speaketh mysteries."* He then makes it clear that it's the Holy Spirit praying to God when you pray in an unknown tongue in *1 Corinthians 14:14–15 (KJV), "For if I pray in an unknown tongue, my spirit prayeth, but my understanding is unfruitful. What is it then? I will pray with the spirit, and I will pray with the understanding also: I will sing with the spirit, and I will sing with the understanding also."*

When Apostle Paul mentions praying with your understanding what that means is praying with your natural language also, whether its English, Hebrew, Spanish, etc. Your understanding is your natural language you speak with on a day-to-day basis in life. Apostle Paul also mentions in *1 Corinthians 14* about praying that you may be able to interpret your own unknown tongue, when he says in *1 Corinthians 14:13 (KJV), "Wherefore let him that speaketh in an unknown tongue pray that he may interpret."* Sometimes when you are praying in an unknown tongue (the Holy Spirit), you may be able to hear the understanding of it in your natural language in your own mind.

Although you are not speaking in your own understanding, sometimes, God gives you the interpretation of it in your own mind as you speak in an unknown tongue out of your mouth. So it is a mental interpretation of it in your own mind. So Apostle Paul tells us to pray that God would give us the interpretation of it so that we may be able to understand what we are exactly praying to God. So we can now see that there is a difference between speaking in diverse tongues and the prayer language of the Holy Spirit. They are both different types of tongues.

Praying in the Holy Spirit as Our Intercessor Can Help Our Weaknesses

Another thing that praying in the Holy Spirit can do is help our "infirmities" or "weaknesses." Apostle Paul mentions in *Romans 8:26–27* that praying in the Holy Spirit can help our "infirmities" when he says in *Romans 8:26–27, "Likewise the Spirit also helpeth our infirmities: for we know not what we should pray for as we ought: but the Spirit itself maketh intercession for us with groanings which cannot be uttered. And he that searcheth the hearts knoweth what is the mind of the Spirit,*

*because he maketh intercession for the saints according to the will
of God."* Although if you look at the Greek word there for
"infirmities" in *Romans 8:26,* it is "astheneia" and it means
"want of strength, weakness, illness, suffering, calamity,
frailty." So it means our weaknesses that we all have.

We all have weaknesses in our life that we need help
with on a day-to-day basis. We also know that the Bible says
in *Hebrews 4* that we can come before the throne of grace
to help us with our infirmities or weaknesses in our time of
need when it says in *Hebrews 4:14–16 (KJV)*, *"Seeing then
that we have a great high priest, that is passed into the heavens,
Jesus the Son of God, let us hold fast our profession. For we have
not an high priest which cannot be touched with the feeling of
our infirmities; but was in all points tempted like as we are,
yet without sin. Let us therefore come boldly unto the throne of
grace, that we may obtain mercy, and find grace to help in time
of need."*

As we all know, Jesus is our mediator to Father God
Jehovah, we can read that in *1 Timothy 2:5 (KJV)*, *"For
there is one God, and one mediator between God and men, the
man Christ Jesus."* Although the Holy Spirit in us intercedes
through Christ and Christ intercedes on our behalf to Father
God Jehovah.

The reason for that is because the Father gave us the
Holy Spirit through Christ, when we first accepted Jesus as
our Lord and Savior. Jesus said in *John 14* that He would
give us another "Comforter" or the Holy Spirit when He
said in *John 14:16–18 (KJV)*, *"And I will pray the Father, and
he shall give you another Comforter, that he may abide with
you for ever; Even the Spirit of truth; whom the world cannot
receive, because it seeth him not, neither knoweth him: but ye
know him; for he dwelleth with you, and shall be in you. I will
not leave you comfortless: I will come to you."* When you look

at the Greek word there for Comforter in *John 14:16 (KJV)*, it is the word *parakletos* and it means "one who pleads another's cause before a judge, a pleader, counsel for defense, legal assistant, an advocate, one who pleads another's cause with one, an intercessor." So the Holy Spirit intercedes to Father God Jehovah on our behalf through Christ Jesus our Lord and Savior.

It is a three-step process: the Holy Spirit intercedes through us to Christ, and Christ intercedes for us to the Father. We can look back again at *Romans 8:26–27* to see that the Holy Spirit intercedes through us on our behalf to the Father. Although that is because of Christ who gave us the Holy Spirit from Father God Jehovah. So the Holy Spirit intercedes for us to Christ who intercedes for us to Father God Jehovah.

It is like a court system. The Holy Spirit bears witness on our behalf to the attorney Jesus and the attorney or Jesus takes our case before the judge or Father God Jehovah. Make sense? That's how it works in the cases of our lives.

Praying in the Holy Spirit Builds Our Faith and Keeps Us in the Love of God

In *Jude 1:20–21,* Jude says that praying in the Holy Spirit can build our faith and keep us in the love of God when he says in *Jude 1:20–21 (KJV), "But ye, beloved, building up yourselves on your most holy faith, praying in the Holy Ghost, Keep yourselves in the love of God, looking for the mercy of our Lord Jesus Christ unto eternal life."* I will say this, I am a true witness to this scripture because when I pray in the Holy Spirit, it builds my faith tremendously because you feel the overwhelming presence of Father God Jehovah just take hold of you and your situation you're going through. It brings the Word of God to life and brings the fullness of your relationship with Christ alive and to its fullness! I'll also say you will notice the longer you pray in the Holy Spirit, the more time will feel like it starts to stand still.

It's almost like you feel a little bit of the stillness and peace of eternity in New Jerusalem down on earth! You will start praying and lose track of all time as you pray intimately with the Father. Your joy in Christ will increase to its fullness, you will have such an addiction to the Holy Spirit, the Lord Jesus, Father God Jehovah, and His Word. You also will begin to see the Word of God come alive and reveal itself to you like it never has before. Also you will begin to receive new revelations in God's Word like you never have before as the Word starts to jump out at you as if you were in it yourself.

As for me, my favorite part of the day is when I get to pray in the Holy Spirit and read Father God Jehovah's Word to see what He has to say every day! I am completely addicted to the Holy Spirit, the Lord Jesus, Father God Jehovah, and His Word! I absolutely cannot get enough of it! I have experienced the Shekinah glory atmosphere in my own room as my room got almost like a little white hazy cloud in it as I prayed in the Holy Spirit more and more.

I sometimes will come into my room and automatically feel the presence of the Holy Spirit before I even start praying! It is absolutely amazing what the Holy Spirit Himself will do when you get in His presence more and more! So in *Jude 1:20–21 (KJV)* when Jude says praying in the Holy Spirit builds your faith and keeps you in the love of God? It absolutely without any doubt will do it!

The Comforter and Spirit of Truth role of the Holy Spirit mentioned in *John 14:16–18 (KJV)* by the Lord Jesus will begin to completely take hold of your situation, in peace and in the truth of the Holy Spirit, the Lord Jesus, Father God Jehovah, and His Word!

Praying and Singing in the Holy Spirit to Worship Father God Jehovah and the Lord Jesus

In this chapter, I want to say that Our Lord Jesus said in *John 4* that we as believers would worship the Father in spirit and in truth when He said in *John 4:23–24 (KJV)*, *"But the hour cometh, and now is, when the true worshippers shall worship the Father in spirit and in truth: for the Father seeketh such to worship him. God is a Spirit: and they that worship him must worship him in spirit and in truth."* I also want to mention that Apostle Paul also said in *1 Corinthians 14* that he would pray in the Holy Spirit but also sing in the Holy Spirit to Father God Jehovah and the Lord Jesus also when He said in *1 Corinthians 14:15 (KJV)*, *"What is it then? I will pray with the spirit, and I will pray with the understanding also: I will sing with the spirit, and I will sing with the understanding also."* So with that being said we as believers can also worship Father God Jehovah, the Lord Jesus, and the Holy Spirit also by singing in the Holy Spirit to them. Sometimes, you just want to worship in the Holy Spirit to Father God Jehovah, the Lord Jesus, and the Holy Spirit, just to be in the presence of Christ and the Father.

So in those occasions singing in the Spirit can help you to just be in the presence of Christ and Father God Jehovah just by worshiping and singing to them in the Holy Spirit. I know for me sometimes I just want to be in the presence of Christ and the Father, so I will sing and worship them in the Holy Spirit just to be in their presence. Also, in those occasions, it can then sometimes turn into a new revelation that

I'll receive in the Word, just by worshipping Christ and the Father in the Holy Spirit.

Praying in the Holy Spirit to Be Renewed in the Spirit of Our Mind

Sometimes we need to be renewed in the spirit of our mind to renew us in the mind of Christ. In *Ephesians 4*, it talks about being renewed in the Spirit of our minds when it says in *Ephesians 4:23–24 (KJV)*, *"And be renewed in the spirit of your mind; And that ye put on the new man, which after God is created in righteousness and true holiness."* On some occasions, we need have our mind restored in the mind of the Holy Spirit and in the mind of Christ when we may be having certain unwanted thoughts trying to attack us and distract us from Christ. So in those occasions we need to pray in the Holy Spirit to renew us in the mind of Christ.

For scripture says in *1 Corinthians 2* that we have the mind of Christ, when it says in *1 Corinthians 2:16 (KJV)*, *"For who hath known the mind of the Lord, that he may instruct him? but we have the mind of Christ."* In those occasions, you will notice that after you pray in the Holy Spirit for some time, you will start to notice the power of God to take over and your mind will start to become clearer and refocused on Christ instead of the thoughts that were trying to attack you and distract you from Christ. We also know that Apostle Paul said in 2 Corinthians that we can bring every thought to the obedience of Christ when he said in *2 Corinthians 10:5 (KJV)*, *"Casting down imaginations, and every high thing that exalteth itself against the knowledge of God, and bringing into captivity every thought to the obedience of Christ."* We are constantly on guard against the devil's schemes and attacks and praying in the Holy Spirit brings the power of God to conquer those attacks and schemes formed against us, for we know that no weapon formed against us shall prosper.

"No weapon that is formed against thee shall prosper; and every tongue that shall rise against thee in judgment thou shalt condemn. This is the heritage of the servants of the Lord, and their righteousness is of me, saith the Lord." (Isaiah 54:17, KJV)

Another scripture that we know talks about being renewed in your mind is in Romans 12 when it says in *Romans 12:2 (KJV), "And be not conformed to this world: but be ye transformed by the renewing of your mind, that ye may prove what is that good, and acceptable, and perfect, will of God."* So we can see that we constantly need to be renewed in the mind of the Holy Spirit, which is the mind of Christ and the Father, to keep us from all the enemy's attacks on a day to day basis.

Speaking in Unknown Tongues in the Church

Apostle Paul knew the importance of speaking in tongues in the church when he said in *1 Corinthians 14:39 (KJV), "Wherefore, brethren, covet to prophesy, and forbid not to speak with tongues."* Although he also knew there had to be order in the church as well. If you look at 1 Corinthians 14, Apostle Paul talked about the order of speaking in unknown tongues in the church when he said in *1 Corinthians 14:27– 28 (KJV), "If any man speak in an unknown tongue, let it be by two, or at the most by three, and that by course; and let one interpret. But if there be no interpreter, let him keep silence in the church; and let him speak to himself, and to God."* When Apostle Paul talks about letting one person interpret, he is referring to one of the nine gifts of the Holy Spirit which

is interpretation of tongues mentioned in *1 Corinthians
12:7–11*. There are people that have the gift of interpreting
unknown tongues so that they may understand what is being
said to the church or to an individual person.

Sometimes, there may be a prophetic message that
is being prayed for the church or for an individual person
when someone is praying in an unknown tongue, and in
those cases, a person who has the gift of interpretation of
tongues is needed to translate that message to the church or
to that individual person. That is why Apostle Paul said in 1
Corinthians 14:27–28 (KJV) if there is not an interpreter let
him keep silence in the church, and let him speak to himself,
and to God. If you remember in 1 Corinthians 14:2, Apostle
Paul talked about how he that speaks in an unknown tongue
speaks mysteries in the Spirit when he said in *1 Corinthians
14:2 (KJV), "For he that speaketh in an unknown tongue speaketh not unto men, but unto God: for no man understandeth
him; howbeit in the spirit he speaketh mysteries."* Those mysteries spoken in the Holy Spirit can sometimes be a prophetic
message to the church or to an individual person that is then
why an interpreter would be needed.

Praying in the Holy Spirit Can Bring You Comfort

When you pray in the Holy Spirit, you will notice the
Comforter role of the Holy Spirit of Christ start to take you
over and bring you comfort and rest. Again, Jesus said that
the Holy Spirit would bring us comfort when he said in *John
14:16–18 (KJV), "And I will pray the Father, and he shall give
you another Comforter, that he may abide with you for ever;
Even the Spirit of truth; whom the world cannot receive, because*

it seeth him not, neither knoweth him: but ye know him; for he dwelleth with you, and shall be in you. I will not leave you comfortless: I will come to you." The more time you spend praying in the Holy Spirit, the more you will feel the comfort of His presence. He brings you refreshing, comfort, and rest from whatever situation you may be in.

You will feel a surge of love through your entire body that is unlike any other love we know. As we know the Word says in *1 John 4:16 (KJV), "And we have known and believed the love that God hath to us. God is love; and he that dwelleth in love dwelleth in God, and God in him."*

Chapter Conclusion

So in conclusion with that being said, praying in the Holy Spirit can bring you comfort, rest, renewal of your mind, prophetic revelations through the word and through speaking in mysteries, help our weaknesses, build our faith, and keep us in the love of God! Also for those of you who have not experienced the prayer language of the Holy Spirit? I would encourage you to spend some intimate time in prayer with Christ and the Father, and just ask them to reveal the prayer language of the Holy Spirit to you. Trust me, it will change your relationship with the Father, the Lord Jesus, and the Holy Spirit forever and for the better.

Praying in the Holy Spirit to Build Your Faith

> *"But ye, beloved, building up yourselves on your most holy faith, praying in the Holy Ghost, Keep yourselves in the love of God, looking for the mercy of our Lord Jesus Christ unto eternal life." (Jude 1:20–21, KJV)*

Conclusion

How to Receive Salvation

THE LORD JESUS IS knocking at the door, guys! So if you feel like you are one of the ones the Lord Jesus is calling today, then what I want you to do right now, guys, is just say a quick prayer with me right now and just say, "God, I come before you today as a humble sinner, and, God, I know I can't make it in this world alone. So right now, God, I just ask and receive your one and only begotten son, the Lord Jesus Christ, to come into my heart today! And, God, I acknowledge and believe that you gave your one and only begotten son to die on the cross for me, for the washing away of my sins, that I may receive eternal life with u some day in heaven! And, God, I also acknowledge and believe that you raised your one and only son, the Lord Jesus Christ, up on the third day from the tomb, and that He is the one and only Savior of the world, and that He is the only way, truth, and the life! And so, God, I just pray all these things right now,

in the name of the Father, the Son, and the Holy Ghost! In Jesus's precious name, Amen!"
For God so loved the world!

> *"For God so loved the world, that he gave his only begotten Son, that whosoever believeth in him should not perish, but have everlasting life. For God sent not his Son into the world to condemn the world; but that the world through him might be saved. He that believeth on him is not condemned: but he that believeth not is condemned already, because he hath not believed in the name of the only begotten Son of God. And this is the condemnation, that light is come into the world, and men loved darkness rather than light, because their deeds were evil. For every one that doeth evil hateth the light, neither cometh to the light, lest his deeds should be reproved. But he that doeth truth cometh to the light, that his deeds may be made manifest, that they are wrought in God." (John 3:16–21, KJV)*

That if you shall confess with your mouth the Lord Jesus, and shalt believe in your heart that God has raised him from the dead, you shall be saved!

> *"That if thou shalt confess with thy mouth the Lord Jesus, and shalt believe in thine heart that God hath raised him from the dead, thou shalt be saved. For with the heart man believeth unto righteousness; and*

with the mouth confession is made unto salvation. For the scripture saith, Whosoever believeth on him shall not be ashamed. For there is no difference between the Jew and the Greek: for the same Lord over all is rich unto all that call upon him. For whosoever shall call upon the name of the Lord shall be saved." (Romans 10:9–13, KJV)

If you have prayed this prayer today and accepted Jesus as your Savior, I would encourage you to get connected with a local church and be baptized as public act of obedience to Christ. As an example to us, Jesus was baptized in the Jordan River by John the Baptist (Matthew 3:13-17; Mark 1:9-11; Luke 3:21-22). Our baptism symbolizes our "old man" dying with Christ and our "new man" resurrected with Him in newness of life through the Holy Spirit (see Acts 2:38-39, KJV). *"Know ye not, that so many of us as were baptized into Jesus Christ were baptized into his death? Therefore we are buried with him by baptism into death: that like as Christ was raised up from the dead by the glory of the Father, even so we also should walk in newness of life. For if we have been planted together in the likeness of his death, we shall be also in the likeness of his resurrection: Knowing this, that our old man is crucified with him, that the body of sin might be destroyed, that henceforth we should not serve sin." (Romans 6:3-6, KJV)*

Begin today in a new life that emulates Christ in every way. A life of faith, courage, hope, love and joy.

"The grace of the Lord Jesus Christ, and the love of God, and the communion of the Holy Ghost, be with you all. Amen." (2 Corinthians 13:14, KJV)

ABOUT THE AUTHOR

TAKING UP YOUR CROSS is John T. Martin's first book. For the past five years, he has had an online ministry through social media including Instagram and twitter @thelastdays777. His ministry has over 17,000 followers worldwide. He is passionate about relating current events with Bible prophecy while bringing the good news of the gospel at the same time. John Martin was born and raised and resides in Franklin, Tennessee.

CPSIA information can be obtained
at www.ICGtesting.com
Printed in the USA
BVHW081447270819
556814BV00005B/1025/P